Letter's Day Out

Learn and Color

By
S. Ketki

BLUEROSE PUBLISHERS
India | U.K.

Copyright © Ketki Shiradhonkar 2024

All rights reserved by author. No part of this publication may be reproduced, stored in a retrieval system or transmitted in any form or by any means, electronic, mechanical, photocopying, recording or otherwise, without the prior permission of the author. Although every precaution has been taken to verify the accuracy of the information contained herein, the publisher assume no responsibility for any errors or omissions. No liability is assumed for damages that may result from the use of information contained within.

BlueRose Publishers takes no responsibility for any damages, losses, or liabilities that may arise from the use or misuse of the information, products, or services provided in this publication.

For permissions requests or inquiries regarding this publication, please contact:

BLUEROSE PUBLISHERS
www.BlueRoseONE.com
info@bluerosepublishers.com
+91 8882 898 898
+4407342408967

ISBN: 978-93-6783-886-0

First Edition: December 2024

Apple

Ball

Cat

Duck

Elephant

Fish

Giraffe

Hen

Ice Cream

Jam

Kite

Lion

Monkey

Newspaper

Octopus

Penguin

Queen

Rabbit

Sun

Train

Umbrella

Violin

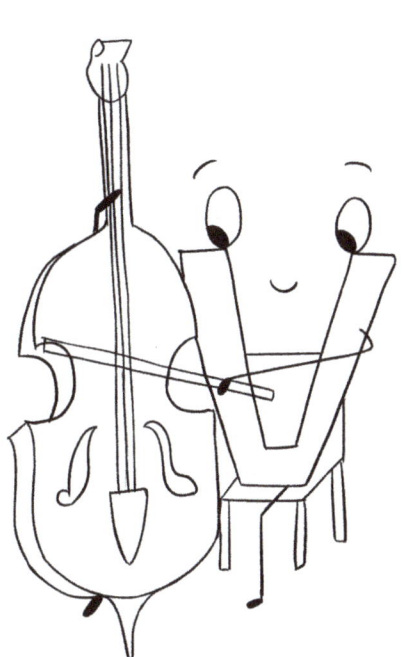

Whale

X-mas Tree

YAK

Zebra

Uppercase Letters

A	N
B	O
C	P
D	Q
E	R
F	S
G	T
H	U
I	V
J	W
K	X
L	Y
M	Z

Lowercase Letters

a	n
b	o
c	p
d	q
e	r
f	s
g	t
h	u
i	v
j	w
k	x
l	y
m	z

Uppercase and Lowercase Letters

A a	N n
B b	O o
C c	P p
D d	Q q
E e	R r
F f	S s
G g	T t
H h	U u
I i	V v
J j	W w
K k	X x
L l	Y y
M m	Z z

www.ingramcontent.com/pod-product-compliance
Lightning Source LLC
LaVergne TN
LVHW070525070526
838199LV00072B/6700